D1715343

JOHN BARCLAY ARMSTRONG

ARMSTRONG AS A SPECIAL RANGER, CIRCA 1889.
Courtesy Tobin Armstrong

JOHN BARCLAY ARMSTRONG
TEXAS RANGER

By Judy Alter

b

BRIGHT SKY PRESS
ALBANY, TEXAS

THE ARMSTRONG FAMILY, CIRCA 1890. TOP ROW FROM LEFT: JOHN B., HOLDING CHARLES ON HIS LAP; JULIA; JOSEPHINE; "GRANNY" DURST; JAMIE; MOLLIE HOLDING ELLIOTT TIM. SEATED IN FRONT IS JOHN.
Courtesy Tobin Armstrong

Bright Sky Press
Box 416, Albany, Texas 76430

Printed in China through Asia Pacific Offset

10   9   8   7   6   5   4   3   2   1

Library of Congress Cataloging-in-Publication Data

Alter, Judy, 1938-
John Barclay Armstrong, Texas Ranger / by Judy Alter.
        p. cm.
ISBN 978-1-931721-86-8 (jacketed hardcover : alk. paper)
1. Armstrong, John B., 1850–1913.
2. Texas Rangers—Biography. I. Title.

HV7911.A76A58 2007
363.2092—dc22
[B]

2007005623

EDITED BY CYNTHIA SELLMAN MENDEZ
BOOK AND JACKET DESIGN BY JULIE SAVASKY
COVER ILLUSTRATION BY CLAUDIA WOLF

TABLE OF CONTENTS

JOHN B. ARMSTRONG AS A YOUNG MAN, PROBABLY IN THE MID-1870S.
Courtesy Tobin Armstrong

Chapter One

JOHN B. ARMSTRONG
MOVES TO TEXAS

John Barclay Armstrong was a lieutenant in the Texas Rangers, a marshal, a rancher, and civic leader. He played an important role in the development of the ranching country of South Texas, but he is best remembered for capturing outlaw John Wesley Hardin.

Like most Texas Rangers, Armstrong was not a native of the state. He was born in McMinnville, Tennessee, on New Year's Day 1850. He was one of six children in the family. His father, also John Barclay, was a physician. Because his father was a prominent citizen with some wealth, young John received a better education than many boys of the day. But he did not want to follow in his father's footsteps as a physician.

Armstrong's middle name has been spelled Barkley, Barcly, and Barclay. His descendants today spell the name Barclay, and that is used throughout this book.

Like many young men after the Civil War, he left home at a young age to find his fortune out West. Reconstruction dominated southern life. Northerners, known as carpetbaggers, controlled the government and the banks, Union troops occupied most towns, and the easy southern way of life was gone.

Armstrong stayed a short while in Missouri and Arkansas. In 1871, he settled in Austin, Texas. No one knows how he earned a living, but he soon became a well-known member of the Travis Rifles. The Rifles were organized in 1873 as an independent infantry military company to protect Austin against Indian attacks. By 1871, the possibility of an Indian attack on a city the size of Austin was unlikely. Nonetheless, the rifle company had forty-five members. They ordered uniforms and put regular notices of their meetings in the newspaper.

The Travis Rifles, however, were mostly a social group. They sponsored competitions modeled after the tournaments of knights in medieval England and competed for prizes in horsemanship and shooting. Many of the townspeople enjoyed the competition, particularly the young ladies of Austin.

After one shooting competition, the Travis Rifles marched in parade uniform down Congress Avenue in the center of Austin. An elaborate lunch with champagne followed the competition. A month later, in November 1873, the ladies of Austin gave a dinner in honor of the members of the rifle group.

Mollie Durst was one of the young ladies who watched the Rifles competitions. Armstrong noticed her immediately and was attracted to her. His interest was returned, but he did not feel that he was in a position to take a wife, so the couple remained friends. Mollie wanted to create a flag for the Travis Rifles but knew she would need the help of other ladies of Austin. Several joined her, and the flag was presented to the group in an elaborate ceremony.

The Travis Rifles were called to business at least once, when Governor E.J. Davis needed them for his personal protection.

Before becoming governor, Davis lived in Texas with his wife and sons and had been a close friend of Sam Houston. But when war came, Davis left the state and joined the Union Army. After the war, he returned and was elected governor in 1869, but he was not a popular official. He believed in strong punishment for those who had voted for secession. He established the State Police and instructed it to punish those who opposed Reconstruction.

In 1873, Governor Davis was defeated for re-election by Richard Coke. Davis refused to give up his office and ordered the Travis Rifles to protect him. The Rifles disobeyed, however, and supported Governor Coke. Armstrong stood guard at the state capitol all night at one point during his duties, but nothing disturbed the peace. The Rifles won praise for their service.

In 1874, Armstrong was asked to run for city marshal on the Democratic ticket, even though he was only twenty-four years old. He pledged to devote himself to the duties of the office, if elected. But he was defeated.

Governor Coke established the Frontier Battalion

"They ride like Mexicans; trail like Indians; shoot like Tennesseans; and fight like the devil." A description of the Texas Rangers attributed to Ranger John Salmon "Rip" Ford.

to protect the Texas boundaries. He also established a force to deal with problems inside Texas. Captain Leander McNelly was in charge of the second group. McNelly was a Confederate veteran who had served in Davis' State Police. Armstrong joined McNelly's unit on April 1, 1875. By joining McNelly's unit, Armstrong became part of the famed Texas Rangers.

MAJOR AND FOUR TEXAS RANGER CAPTAINS, CIRCA 1900.
STANDING FROM LEFT: JOHN A. BROOKS, JOHN H. ROGERS, UNIDENTIFIED.
SEATED FROM LEFT: LAMARTINE PEMBERTON "LAM" SIEKER,
JOHN B. ARMSTRONG, WILLIAM J. MCDONALD. THE UNIDENTIFIED STANDING
FIGURE AT RIGHT MAY BE ADJ. GEN. W.H. MABRY OR A MAN NAMED WAITE;
IT IS DEFINITELY NOT J.B. GILLETT, AS HAS SOMETIMES BEEN CLAIMED.
Courtesy Haley Memorial Library and History Center, Midland, Texas

Chapter Two

THE TEXAS RANGERS

As a member of the Texas Rangers, Armstrong belonged to one of the oldest state law enforcement agencies in the United States. The agency traced its beginnings back to 1823 when empresario Stephen F. Austin organized two companies "for the common defense." Austin's Colony was large. Its six or seven hundred settlers lived in widely scattered cabins. With no close neighbors, families were easy targets for attacks by Indians and bandits from deep in Mexico. (Texas was then part of Mexico.) Austin organized the two companies to protect his settlers. They became known as Rangers because their duties caused them to "range," or travel, over the countryside. But in the 1820s there was not yet any formal organization called the Texas Rangers.

In 1835, Austin organized a council to govern the Rangers and oversee their activities. On October 17, the council approved a resolution creating a group formally known as the Texas Rangers. There were about sixty men in the authorized "ranging companies." When Texas declared its independence from Mexico, the temporary government approved the establishment of the Rangers.

Rangers served as scouts during the Texas Revolution, when Texians fought for freedom from Mexico. They carried messages between branches of the struggling Texas Army. When Texians fled Santa Anna's army in the flight that became known as the Runaway Scrape, Texas Rangers protected the fleeing people.

By 1836, after the fight for freedom from Mexico ended, the Rangers numbered almost three hundred. General Sam Houston became the first president of the Republic of Texas. He did not think he needed the Rangers, and they were not often called upon for service.

Mirabeau B. Lamar followed Houston and became the second president of the Republic. He had different plans and ideas for Texas than Houston. While Houston had been friendly with the Cherokee Indians who lived in Northeast

The Runaway Scrape happened after the fall of the Alamo. General Sam Houston marched his troops east, away from Mexican General Santa Anna. Houston did not confront Santa Anna because he needed time to train his army. Santa Anna's troops followed. As they fled the Mexican troops, people left behind their homes, livestock, and belongings. Whole towns were left empty, and many were burned to the ground. The people walked, rode horseback, or rode in carts in the rain, mud, and cold. They finally were able to return home after Houston defeated Santa Anna at the Battle of San Jacinto, but for many, there were no homes left.

Texas — having once lived with the tribe and been married to a Cherokee woman — Lamar disliked Indians and wanted them all out of Texas. He used the Rangers in his war against the Indians. After the battle at the Neches River in East Texas, the Cherokee were driven from Texas to the Indian Territory (present-day Oklahoma). Lamar had less success against the Comanche, who continued to attack settlers until the 1880s.

In 1840, the Rangers were part of three events in Texas history: the Council House Fight, the raid on Linville, and the Battle of Plum Creek.

The Council House Fight in San Antonio began after Comanche leaders were summoned to peace talks to discuss Indian captives. A peaceful chief of the Comanche brought several captives. One of them was Mathilda Lockhart, whose nose had been burned off. The sight enraged white leaders, who demanded the release of all Comanche captives. The chief tried to explain that he had no control over bands of Comanche other than his own. He did not convince the white leaders, who had the Indians arrested. Then, inside and outside the Council House, fighting began. Thirty-five Comanche were killed, including women and children. Seven Texans also died as the Indians carried the fight throughout the streets of San Antonio.

The Comanche sought revenge by raiding the town of Linville, on the Gulf Coast. They even waded into the water to chase settlers trying to get away in boats. The Indians destroyed the town and fled north. They were stopped by Texas Rangers and others at Plum Creek. There, the Indians were defeated and lost many warriors, women, and children.

Sam Houston was re-elected in 1841. He had seen how effective the Rangers were and approved a law that officially organized the Rangers to protect the southern and western frontiers of Texas. Captain John Coffee "Jack" Hays was in charge. With Houston's approval, the Rangers protected white settlers against Indian attacks and helped stop invasions of outlaws from Mexico. Under Hays' direction, the quality of the Rangers improved. He had strict requirements about who could become a Ranger. He also began a training program.

In December of 1845, Texas became a state in the Union. That year, the Mexican-American War also began. It would eventually establish a permanent boundary between Texas and Mexico. Rangers were so successful in fighting Mexican guerillas that they became known by them as *"los diablos,"* or "the devils."

Captain John Salmon "Rip" Ford led a company of Rangers during the Mexican-American War. He described his men as a "company of sober and brave men." They were, he said, mostly unmarried. Only a few drank whiskey. They did not gallop through the streets, shooting and yelling, as many cowboys did. They "did right because it was right."

During the Civil War, which lasted from 1861 to 1865, the Rangers almost disappeared. The state had no money to pay them. Many Rangers fought in the Civil War on battlefields far from Texas. With many men away, women and children were left home alone. They were easy targets for Indian attacks on the Texas frontier. When Indian attacks threatened, they left their farms and moved into settlements for the protection and comfort of other settlers. Volunteers took up arms and called themselves rangers as they patrolled the settlements, but they were not part of the legally organized Texas Rangers.

Reconstruction followed the defeat of the South. Northerners who remained angry about the war forced unpopular laws on southern states. The Rangers ceased to exist, even on paper. Reconstruction Governor E.J. Davis used his State Police force to enforce unpopular laws. That force was modeled on the Rangers.

In the 1870s, Texas began to govern itself again. The state government appropriated $75,000 to organize six companies of seventy-five Rangers each. Indians had been raiding the western frontier, outlaws were committing robbery and murder throughout the state, and Mexican and Anglo raiders from Mexico were driving stolen Texas cattle back across the border. Clearly, law enforcement was needed. This is when Captain Leander McNelly's company of Rangers, patrolling the Nueces Strip in South Texas, became legendary.

The phrase "One Riot, One Ranger" also has its legend. A generally believed story is that the

The Nueces Strip is the land between the Nueces River and the Rio Grande. It is bordered on the east by the Gulf Coast. Thorny brush such as mesquite, cactus, agarita, and yucca covered much of the land. For many years, in this sparsely populated region, outlaws roamed freely. Other names for this region are Wild Horse Desert or *El Desierto de Muerto* (The Desert of the Dead).

Rangers were called upon to stop a riot in a town. When the train arrived that was carrying the lone Ranger, outraged citizens demanded to know if there weren't more men. The Ranger is reported to have said, "You only got one riot, don't you?"

Chapter Three

JOHN B. ARMSTRONG'S CAREER AS A RANGER

After signing with McNelly's Rangers, Armstrong was quickly promoted to sergeant, perhaps because of his service with the Travis Rifles. He did not have to wait long to be called into duty.

Thirty or more raiders from Mexico had ridden into Nueces County, and they were headed for the city of Corpus Christi. Thomas Noakes, owner of a store and post office, resisted and killed one raider. But his business was burned to the ground. Ranchers became vigilantes. They captured and lynched one raider. Then they rode into Mexico, burning ranches and killing Mexican citizens on both sides of the border. Rancher Richard King asked the governor to send forces to restore law

Richard King was the owner of the King Ranch, considered one of the largest ranches in Texas. King was the first to see the possibilities of raising cattle in the Nueces Strip. Today the renowned King Ranch is still run by descendants of the founder.

and order, and McNelly's unit was sent.

McNelly disbanded the vigilantes and developed a spy system. His men, however, were impatient. They wanted action. Armstrong had briefly returned to San Antonio and Austin but was back in the Nueces Strip in time for the first important battle with the raiders. The Rangers confronted sixteen raiders who had about three hundred head of cattle. All the raiders were killed. Only one Ranger was lost. This was the battle at Palo Alto Prairie or *Las Cuevas*.

McNelly defied treaties between the United States and Mexico by crossing the border to recover cattle and kill the thieves. His rangers returned cattle to several ranchers, including Richard King. The bloody battles were mostly on the Mexican side of the border. In one, Armstrong and another man were left afoot when their horses panicked and pitched them. During these battles, Armstrong demonstrated such courage and determination that he was given the nickname, "McNelly's Bulldog."

In June 1876, McNelly's Rangers arrested John King Fisher, a thief and killer from Dimmit County in the Nueces Strip. Fisher was one of many outlaws who found safe haven in the Strip. Northwestern Dimmit County was known as King Fisher Territory. During this time, Armstrong had often been in charge of small squads sent on special duty. He led a squad to San Patricio to investigate the killing of an ex-sheriff. In September 1876, he was sent to Espantosa Lake to round up a camp of outlaws from the King Fisher gang and possibly King Fisher himself. They did not find Fisher, but they killed a number of outlaws who resisted arrest. They also recovered stolen cattle and oxen. The story of Armstrong's bravery at Espantosa Lake was carried in many Texas newspapers.

During his years with the Rangers, Armstrong was described as a large man with a blond moustache and goatee. He stood straight and tall and sat a horse gracefully. He was in his late twenties.

Late in 1876, McNelly's health was failing from tuberculosis. He was unable to lead his men, and Armstrong took on more and more responsibility. He was, however, passed over as McNelly's successor in favor of Lieutenant J.L. Hall. Armstrong was promoted to second lieutenant and continued leading scouts, arresting wanted men in the Strip.

Chapter Four

THE CAPTURE OF
JOHN WESLEY HARDIN

John Wesley Hardin began his life of crime in 1867 in high school, when he stabbed another boy to death. At fifteen, he quarreled with a black man and shot him. He also killed several soldiers. When he went on a cattle drive up the Chisholm Trail, he killed seven people on the way and three in Abilene, Kansas. He married, had two children, and killed four more people before he spent a brief period in jail in Cherokee County, Texas.

Hardin was wanted for killing Comanche County Deputy Charles Webb in May 1874. He was caught in Louisiana and put in a Texas prison, but he escaped and disappeared. Meanwhile, the unit of Texas Rangers led by Captain Leander

> John Wesley Hardin was the
> son of a Methodist preacher,
> schoolteacher, and lawyer.

McNelly was called in to stop the Sutton / Taylor
Feud, in which Hardin was involved. Armstrong
had traced and "captured" Hardin once before—
but the man he and his deputies arrested proved
to be an imposter. He wanted to find the real
outlaw. The Rangers tried unsuccessfully for
several months to end the feud. Armstrong's
determination to capture John Wesley Hardin
began with this effort to stop the feud.

In August 1877, Armstrong was on leave from
the Rangers, recovering from an accidental gunshot
wound. Cleaning his gun, he had shot himself in the
hip. The wound was serious and left Armstrong
walking with a cane. But he asked the Texas
Adjutant General to allow him to go after Hardin
again, in spite of the injury. Permission was granted,
and John Duncan, a detective from Dallas, was
assigned to work with Armstrong.

They tracked Hardin by intercepting a letter
from his wife to one of her relatives in Texas.
Armstrong and Duncan learned that Hardin was
living in Alabama. They asked a judge for an

arrest warrant naming Hardin. They also asked for a warrant using his alias, J.H. Swain. But the two lawmen were so anxious to catch Hardin that they left for Alabama before getting the warrants.

A railroad superintendent in Alabama said Hardin had threatened him, so he was glad to help the Rangers. When they learned that Hardin

The Sutton/Taylor feud was the longest and bloodiest of several Texas feuds after the Civil War. William Sutton was a deputy sheriff and member of the State Police. The Taylor family was known as horse and cattle thieves. Hardin sided with the Taylors. The feud may have started over the killing of soldiers or a disputed horse sale. It pitted the Taylors against members of the Texas State Police, generally under the leadership of William Sutton. The feud's murders, kidnappings, and lynchings happened mostly in DeWitt County. Men were lured from their homes, ambushed and shot. Every time one side killed a man, the other side vowed revenge. It is difficult to be sure how many people died—perhaps as many as twenty-five or thirty.

was in Pensacola, Florida, the superintendent ordered a special train to take Armstrong and Duncan there.

Texas Rangers did not have authority outside Texas. Armstrong asked for help from Sheriff William H. Hutchinson of Escambia County, Florida. Sheriff Hutchinson learned that Hardin would be on a train leaving Pensacola, so he worked with the railroad superintendent to plan a trap.

Hardin boarded the train with four members of his gang. They headed for the smoking car, leaving their shotguns in the overhead rack with their luggage. The five had pistols concealed in their pockets, however. Armstrong was hiding in the baggage car, and Duncan was on the station platform.

At this point, there are several stories of the capture.

The most likely one says that deputies grabbed the unsuspecting Hardin before he could draw his pistol. Armstrong, still recovering from his gunshot wound, switched his cane to his left hand. With his right hand he drew his Colt .45. One of Hardin's companions, Jimmy Mann, saw Armstrong coming and shot at him. The bullet came so close, it creased the Ranger's hat. Armstrong fired one shot, hitting Mann in the heart. Mann dived out the train window and fell dead on the platform.

Another story, however, claims that it was a deputy who shot Mann. Mann had no warrants in his name and would have been freed. He probably believed they were being attacked by robbers. That is what Hardin claimed to have thought at first.

Hardin saw Armstrong with the Colt .45, a weapon the Rangers often used. He called out "Texas, by God!" He kept trying to fight off the deputies so that he could get to his pistol. (Another story says he couldn't fire at Armstrong because his gun was caught in his suspenders!) Armstrong demanded his surrender. Hardin told him to go ahead and shoot. Instead, the Ranger knocked Hardin in the head with his pistol. The outlaw was unconscious for so long that Armstrong was afraid perhaps he had killed him. But eventually, Hardin gained consciousness, and the Ranger signaled the engineer to pull out of the station.

In his 1896 autobiography, *The Life of John Wesley Hardin as Written by Himself,* the outlaw said Armstrong saved his life. "He's too brave to kill," Armstrong is supposed to have said. He threatened to kill the first man who shot Hardin. Hardin did not mention being knocked out. He did say someone kept trying to hit him on the head. Later, he called Armstrong "a Texan of the old school." Hardin said he was never treated better in his life. Hardin's autobiography is available today under the title *Gunfighter.*

The lawmen took Hardin to Montgomery, Alabama. They still did not have warrants. The lawyer Hardin had hired asked the judge to free him. The judge refused. They had to wait in Montgomery for several days. After several telegrams to Texas, the warrants arrived and Armstrong and Duncan took their prisoner back to Texas.

Curious people crowded railroad stations along the way, hoping to get a glimpse of the famous outlaw. Armstrong kept him on the train. In Austin, he secretly took him off the train before it got to the station. He knew that a crowd would be waiting and he wanted to avoid trouble. Hardin later admitted to a great fear of being lynched. He didn't trust the Rangers to protect him.

Back in Texas, Armstrong turned his prisoner over to local authorities and collected the $4,000 award that had been offered. He had captured an outlaw long wanted in Texas. Hardin was said to have committed twenty-seven murders.

Hardin was sentenced to twenty-five years for the killing of Charles Webb in Comanche County. This murder was not connected to the Sutton / Taylor Feud, but Texas officials saw removing Hardin from the scene as one way to end the feud. Hardin tried to escape from jail several times. He also read religious books, studied law, and was superintendent of the prison Sunday school. He was

The motion picture *The Lawless Breed* is based on John Wesley Hardin's life and story. The television series, "Walker, Texas Ranger," featured Chuck Norris as a Texas Ranger superhero. It is now in reruns. The Lone Ranger series, popularized in the 1940s and 1950s, entertained radio, television, and movie audiences. Clayton Moore portrayed the Lone Ranger on the television series, and is best remembered for his portrayal of the masked hero.

pardoned in 1894 and became a lawyer.

After Hardin's capture, Armstrong was the target of an assassination plot by Hardin's friends. The wild scheme involved Mexicans disguised as Indians and freeing persons from all jails, including the jail in Travis County. The threat was never taken seriously. Armstrong was promoted to first lieutenant because of his arrest of Hardin.

The citizens of Austin wanted Armstrong to run for city marshal because of his "gallantry and daring and good judgment in arresting desperate men." He did not want the office and did not want to be involved in politics, so he declined. But in early 1878, he was back in the city to see Mollie Durst.

As the Ranger who captured John Wesley Hardin, Armstrong joined a select list of Rangers who became famous for their brave deeds. Sul Ross defeated Comanche Chief Peta Nocona and his son, Quanah Parker, at the fight at the Pease River and returned white captive Cynthia Ann Parker to her family in East Texas. Leander McNelly became famous for controlling outlaws in the Nueces Strip. Frank Hamer made a name for himself by tracking and ambushing robbers Clyde Barrow and Bonnie Parker.

He felt he now had the reputation and respect to ask her to marry him. They were married on February 20, 1878, with many Rangers attending the ceremony. He was a celebrity, and she was an Austin favorite.

MAJOR ARMSTRONG WITH SONS JOHN AND CHARLEY, CIRCA 1896.
Courtesy Tobin Armstrong

Chapter Five

RANCHER AND CIVIC LEADER

A rmstrong retired from the Texas Rangers at the end of December 1878. He may have felt that the Ranger life kept him away from his wife too much. They were now living with Mollie's mother in Austin, and Mollie was expecting their first child. Maria Josephine was born April 5, 1879.

Armstrong began a career in real estate. He was a clerk for the owners of the Texas Land Agency. His letterhead read: "Office of Jno. B. Armstrong, Dealer in All Kinds of Real Estate & Live Stock & Gen. Com. Agt." He signed his name Jno. B. Armstrong. "Gen. Com. Agt" probably stood for general commission agent.

Armstrong had a good business and was active in community affairs. He was, for instance, a judge for a competition between two drill teams. One team was made up of boys, and the other of girls. The girls carried brooms instead of rifles. The girls won the contest.

Though he was living a very active and full life, Armstrong still yearned to be a rancher. Almost by accident, he learned there was South Texas land in the family. Mollie's father, James Durst, was in the Rangers in the late 1830s. Then he was land commissioner in Nacogdoches County. In 1852, he bought fourteen leagues of La Barreta Grant in Willacy County (the land is now in Kenedy County, which absorbed parts of Willacy) in South Texas. Durst lived in Starr County and represented Starr in the state Senate until 1855. Then he moved his family to South Texas. He became collector of customs at Port Isabel. James Durst died in 1858, when Mollie was only three. Her mother returned to Austin with her children. She left behind thousands of acres of undeveloped land in Willacy County. The land had no fences, no roads, and no law.

The handling of Mollie's father's estate was complicated and apparently dishonest. Some of the land was illegally sold. Mollie's mother never received any money, and the attorneys handling the estate

Mifflin Kenedy was a former partner of rancher Richard King in both the steamship business and a ranching operation in South Texas. Kenedy owned a large ranch and was the first to fence his land. Kenedy, Texas, and Kenedy County are named after him.

held title to the land. In the 1880s, Armstrong knew that the estate had been illegally handled.

It took years to get a clear title, but Armstrong did not wait. He began a ranching operation. Mollie's brother, James, lived on the land to make the claim legal. They had the help of Mifflin Kenedy.

These early ranchers, including King, Kenedy, and Armstrong, developed the Nueces Strip into usable land. They experimented with breeding their domestic cattle with the wild animals known as Spanish cattle. (They would probably be called Longhorns today.) Armstrong followed Kenedy's lead and fenced large sections of his land because of the danger of raiders from Mexico. The King Ranch and the Armstrong Ranch found artesian wells deep in the sandy soil to provide water for their cattle.

Armstrong needed money to run the ranch and to travel to Mexico for documents needed to prove ownership of the land. He also had to pay taxes and pay for fencing the land. He became discouraged and thought about selling the land and living permanently in Austin. He had built a home for his family in the city. His elderly mother was living with them, and he thought it would be difficult for her to make the move. His children were nearing school age. He had doubts about taking his family to the remote, unsettled area.

The appeal of ranching won out, and the family moved to South Texas in 1885. They had three children when they left Austin — four more were born after the move. They lived in a small, one-story house with a front porch. An extension on the back was the kitchen. It was common in those days to separate the kitchen from the main house in case of a cooking fire. Armstrong began work on a real ranch house.

The new house became known as "The Chicago Ranch," although no one knows why. The house was surrounded by jacals which housed the kitchen and dining room. There were two other jacals for the Mexican workers. All the jacals had thatched roofs woven of long native grasses.

Armstrong finally proved fraud by the estate lawyers in 1889, and the land was returned to the Durst and Armstrong families. Later, a new main house was built about ten miles away. The

Armstrong family still lives in that house today.

In 1888, Robert Kleberg of the King Ranch recommended Armstrong for re-enlistment as a

Robert Kleberg, the son of German immigrants, was born in DeWitt County in 1853. He earned a law degree from the University of Virginia and began a law practice in South Texas at Cuero. Eventually he opened offices in Corpus Christi. Richard King became one of his clients and soon learned to trust the young lawyer's ability and judgment. After King's death, his widow, Henrietta King, asked Kleberg to assume management of King Ranch. Kleberg introduced Hereford and Durham shorthorn cattle to the ranch, acquired more land, and drilled artesian wells. He also planned the townsite of Kingsville. As an active member and president of the Texas and Southwestern Cattle Raisers Association, he led the fight against the Texas fever tick. Kleberg married Alice Gertrudis King, and they had five children. Their son, Robert Kleberg, Jr., became manager of the ranch after his father.

"special Ranger" in the Frontier Battalion. Kleberg wrote that South Texas was so remote that sheriffs had no control over outlaws. A sheriff's authority ended at his county line. Outlaws could easily slip from one county to another. Kleberg suggested adding leading citizens of the area as Rangers, without pay. This title gave them the legal right to protect their property and families from outlaws.

The Rangers were often criticized during this time. A former Ranger on the King Ranch found a rustler branding a calf. The rustler shot at the Ranger, and the Ranger killed the rustler. In this case, the shooting was self defense. Many other border Rangers took advantage of their power and killed Mexicans without justification. Many Texans still resented the deaths of Anglos at the Alamo and Goliad during the Texas Revolution. They blamed Mexicans generations later. The Rangers worked constantly to rid the corps of these unqualified men.

Armstrong also repeated his experience with the Travis Rifles, joining the Brownsville Rifles. The Brownsville Rifles did public drill competitions, as the Travis Rifles had. There was a large competition in June 1889 to celebrate Galveston's fiftieth birthday. The Brownsville Rifles took first place and earned a flag valued at $250.

During the 1898 Spanish-American War, Armstrong was lieutenant colonel and assistant chief of ordnance. He preferred to be called Major Armstrong, because during the war, he assumed command of a Texas Volunteer regiment and was given the rank of major by General Charles A. Culberson. He never saw real fighting during that war.

Armstrong joined the King and Kenedy ranches in working with railroads to transport their cattle to market. Previously, cattle had to be driven to Corpus Christi or Brownsville. The Southern Pacific decided it was too expensive to extend their line to South Texas. The ranchers established the St. Louis, Brownsville, and Mexico Railway. By then, Richard King had died. His widow, Henrietta, donated land across King Ranch for a right of way for the train. The train made its first run on July 4, 1904. The occasion was marked by big celebrations with flags and bands. The train traveled from Corpus Christi to Brownsville in nine hours — and then back again. New towns grew along the tracks. One of the largest was Kingsville, on land donated by the Henrietta King. The town of Armstrong was about two miles from the Armstrong ranch house.

After the family had settled into life in south Texas, tragedy struck Armstrong. In December 1897, Mollie contracted rabies from the family dog, at their Austin home. Armstrong was away

> Armstrong's children and grandchildren recalled him as a stern and determined man. Once he was on a railroad car with his daughters. He spoke harshly to two drunken men who were using bad language in loud voices. When they paid no attention, he grabbed each by the hair and banged their heads together. Then he went back to his seat. The men remained quiet.

when she died but hastened back to Austin from the ranch. She was buried from the church in which they were married. Several years later, his oldest son was killed in a horseback accident while herding cattle as his father watched helplessly. In 1912, his mother-in-law, who managed the household after Mollie's death, died. In April 1913, Armstrong became ill with a kidney infection. He died May 1 and was buried near his family members and with all the honors befitting a retired Texas Ranger.

His grandson, John, recalled that once in a carriage headed for the ranch, he did not obey his grandfather's order to "hush up." He was about five years old, but he was put out of the carriage and left alone on the prairie. After a short while, a wagon was sent to bring him back to the ranch.

Chapter Six

THE TEXAS RANGERS TODAY

The capture of John Wesley Hardin was a highlight in the history of the Texas Rangers. So was the fatal wounding of stagecoach robber Sam Bass in Round Rock, Texas.

But when Armstrong left the Rangers, the days of the outlaws were disappearing. The Rangers fell out of the public eye, and there was talk of disbanding them. They didn't seem needed.

In 1914, however, the Rangers were kept busy by the revolution in Mexico. Pancho Villa and other Mexican guerillas raided across the border. Raiders destroyed farms, irrigation systems, and railroad lines. Rangers were charged with restoring order. Special Loyalty Rangers were organized to patrol the border. These Rangers did not always uphold the good reputation that the agency had earned. They bullied the Tejano population. It is estimated that they killed as many as five thousand Hispanics between 1914 and 1919. Their reputation became that of racist, brutal killers. An investigation followed. The number of men in each Ranger unit was cut. Salaries were raised in order to attract a better quality of men.

Governor Miriam "Ma" Ferguson first took office in 1923. She was re-elected in 1932. "Ma" did not like the Rangers. They had supported her opponent for election, former Governor Ross Sterling. Governor Ferguson cut the Rangers to forty-five men during the Depression. But during this time, one of the most dramatic episodes in Ranger history occurred. Former Ranger Frank Hamer tracked and killed Clyde Barrow and Bonnie Parker, leaders of the gang that had committed murders, robberies,

In the spring of 1878, Sam Bass held up four trains within twenty-five miles of Dallas. He was betrayed by one of his own men. The Rangers fought a gun battle with him near Round Rock and found him, wounded, outside the town. He died two days later.

Today, Texas Rangers proudly wear a "star in a wheel" badge. Until the late nineteenth century, Rangers did not wear badges. They have never worn uniforms.

and auto thefts. They had engineered a prison breakout in which a guard was killed. They always escaped law enforcement officials. The State of Texas wanted them brought to justice. Hamer and a small posse trapped the outlaws in Louisiana, peppering their car with 130 rounds of ammunition and killing both outlaws instantly.

In 1935, one hundred years after the first formal organization of the Texas Rangers, the Texas Legislature established the Department of Public Safety. The Rangers became part of that department. Today they are one of the best law enforcement agencies in the world. They protect the governor of Texas, track fugitives, investigate crimes, monitor livestock brands, and keep the peace.

The Texas Ranger Hall of Fame and Museum is located in Waco, Texas. John Barclay Armstrong is a member of the Hall of Fame.

GLOSSARY

ARTESIAN WELL A well in which water rises from beneath a rock layer of the earth's surface because of pressure beneath the surface.

AUTOBIOGRAPHY An account of a person's life written by the person.

CARPETBAGGER A northerner who went south after the Civil War to find political power and take advantage of the lack of organization in the government of southern states. They were called carpetbaggers because they usually carried their belongings in bags made of carpet.

EMPRESARIO One granted land by the Mexican government, with the understanding that he will establish settlements on that land. Much of Texas was settled by empresarios who were granted land by Mexico. Austin's Colony was the largest empresario colony.

FEUD A bitter, prolonged quarrel between individuals or families.

INTERCEPT To stop a letter or message before it reaches the person for whom it is intended.

JACAL A hut with a thatched roof and walls made of thin sticks driven into the ground, plastered over with mud.

LEAGUE A unit of land measure; approximately 3 miles or 4.8 kilometers.

RECONSTRUCTION The period after the Civil War, when southern states had no power and were reorganized for admittance into the Union.

TEXIAN The name used for Texas residents until about the 1850s.

TUBERCULOSIS An infectious disease, caused by bacteria; it can affect any tissue in the body, but most often settles in the lungs; in the 19th century it was also known as consumption.

VIGILANTES Citizens who take the law into their own hands without any authorization.

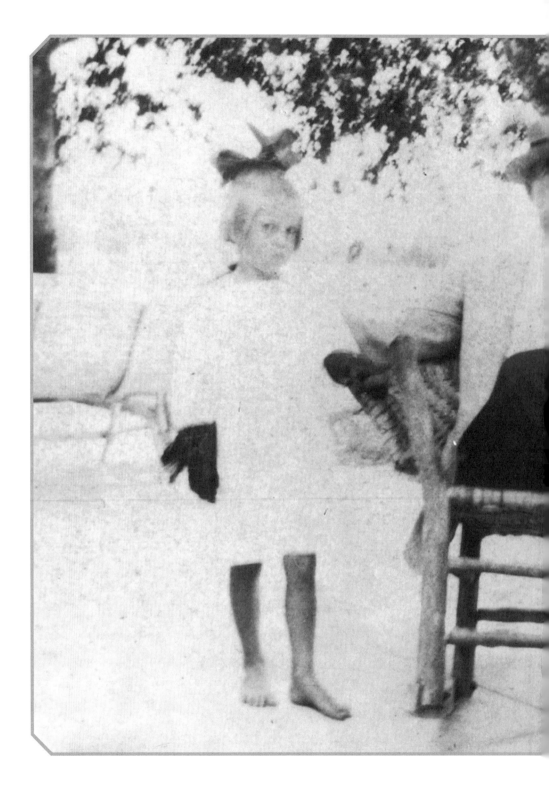

JOHN B. ARMSTRONG RELAXING WITH TWO GRANDCHILDREN,
ELIZABETH BONNEAU BENNETT AND JOHN MIRZA BENNETT JR., CIRCA 1912.
Courtesy Tobin Armstrong

ARMSTRONG TIMELINE

1823 Stephen F. Austin organizes two companies for "the common defense"

1836 Texas Revolution; Fall of the Alamo; Santa Anna defeated at San Jacinto; Texas becomes an independent republic; Sam Houston is elected president

1838 Mirabeau B. Lamar is elected the second president of the Republic of Texas

1841 Houston is elected to second term as president

1845 Texas becomes a state

1846-1848 Mexican-American War

1850 January 1, John Barclay Armstrong is born at McMinnville, Tennessee

1860 Ranger Sul Ross kills Comanche chief Peta Nocona at the Pease River and captures his son, Quanah Parker

1861-1865 The Civil War

1865-1866 Armstrong leaves his family and home to seek his fortune in the West

1866-1875 Sutton/Taylor Feud in East Texas

1871 Armstrong settles in Austin, Texas

1873 Armstrong joins the Travis Rifles; the Travis Rifles defend newly elected Governor Richard Coke when defeated Reconstruction Governor E.J. Davis refuses to leave office.

1874 Armstrong runs for the office of marshal but is defeated

1875 Armstrong joins the Texas Rangers and joins Captain Leander McNelly in fighting outlaws in Texas' Nueces Strip

1876 Armstrong is involved in the arrest of John King Fisher

1877 Armstrong captures John Wesley Hardin

1878 Armstrong marries Mollie Durst in Austin in February and officially resigns from the Texas Rangers in December

1879 Armstrong's daughter, Maria Josephine, is born

LATE 1870S Armstrong discovers his wife's family has ranch land in South Texas

1885 Armstrong moves his family to the ranch

1887 Armstrong enlists as a volunteer in the Frontier Battalion

1888 Armstrong joins the Brownville Rifles; becomes a "special Ranger" in the Frontier Battalion

1897 Mollie Durst Armstrong dies in December

1898 Spanish-American War

1904 St. Louis, Brownsville, and Mexico Railway makes its first run on July 4

1905 Armstrong's oldest son, John Barclay, dies in a horse and cattle accident

1912 Granny Durst, Mollie's mother, dies

1913 John Barclay Armstrong dies on May 1st

1914-1916 Mexican Revolution

1934 Texas Ranger Frank Hamer leads an ambush that kills famous outlaws Bonnie Parker and Clyde Barrow

1935 The Texas Rangers become part of the Department of Public Safety

For Morgan, Sawyer,
Jacob, and Ford